60 Minutes
of **Wisdom**

60 Minutes
of **Wisdom**

DEREK GRIER

60 MINUTES OF WISDOM by Derek Grier
Published by Creation House
A Strang Company
600 Rinehart Road
Lake Mary, Florida 32746
www.creationhouse.com

Design Director: Bill Johnson

Cover Designer: Amanda Potter

Copyright © 2009 by Derek Grier

Library of Congress Control Number: 2009922337
International Standard Book Number: 978-1-59979-724-3

First Edition

09 10 11 12 13 — 9 8 7 6 5 4 3 2 1
Printed in the United States of America

ACKNOWLEDGMENTS

M Y DEEPEST LOVE AND ADMIRATION TO my wife, Yeromitou. Your strength and kindness inspire me. You are a gift from God. Derek and David, thank you for sharing your dad with the demands of minstry. Karen Prewitt, my administrative assistant, thanks for your faithfulness in doing a very tedious and challenging job. Mom and Dad, thanks for your support and encouragement. Shani McKenzie and the Grace Church Working Group, I appreciate your input.

Dr. Myles Munroe, special thanks for being an outstanding mentor. Your wisdom has helped to keep me grounded. Jesus, the more I find out about You, the more I discover myself. Loving you is almost selfish.

CONTENTS

INTRODUCTION

I T IS THE MOMENTS THAT MAKE THE MINUTE and the minutes that make the hour; the strokes of the brush that make the painting and each note that makes the song. It seems all big things come from how we handle small crises and opportunities.

In 2007, my congregation moved from a high school across town and purchased a building in a new neighborhood. Because of the relocation, attendance dropped precipitously, from several hundred to sometimes less than a hundred. We were faced with a new 1.2 million dollar mortgage, cost overruns, and sinking morale. We all prayed for a miracle, but I knew that the answer was to make better use of the resources we already had at our disposal. Bigger is only better, if the smaller is made strong.

Creating a typical half-hour radio or TV program was too expensive for us, at the time. After a night in prayer, I put a second mortgage on my home and decided we could pay for a few sixty-second radio spots. Out of this, the *Ministry Minute* was born.

I had only sixty seconds to give a meaningful, understandable, and memorable message that would deeply impact the life of the listener. In a year's time, over one thousand people visited our church because of the *Ministry Minute*. We have received countless testimonies of how our weekly sixty seconds has changed lives.

My original intent was not to write a book but to simply create God moments for people listening to the radio on their jobs or on the drive to and from work. I had only sixty-second slices of time, for heaven to smack the earth and make issues that were dark and tangled, clear in the hearts of listeners. My prayer is that as you read on, you will have such an experience. May each minute invade future hours; the hours transform your years; all because of the sixty minutes ahead.

Chapter 1

HAPPINESS

Minute 1: Choose to Be Happy

Abraham Lincoln experienced long bouts of depression. He eventually made this statement: "Most people are as happy as they make up their mind to be."[1] If you live long enough, you will discover that true happiness does not come from events alone but from a choice. You have to choose to be happy. The word *happy* derives partly from the word *happenstance*, which connotes that a person's happiness is at the mercy of the stuff that "happens" to us externally. But true joy is internal and comes from a source within.

James 1:2 says, "Consider it pure joy, my brothers, whenever you face trials of many kinds." What does *consider* mean? It means, simply, to think through something until you make a decision. In other words, when we face trials, it is up to us to choose our response. James states further, "Perseverance must finish its work so that you can be mature and complete, not lacking anything" (James 1:4). He promises that only those of us who choose joy can end up mature and complete. We may not be able to control what happens to us, but we can certainly control our response. There are times when we need to cry, but at some point we must dry our eyes and make the choice to go ahead with living.

Minute 2: Finding Our Measure

After a major milestone, I asked myself whether I was finally successful. But as I searched my heart I was stumped because I had never really defined success. I searched for a definition but drew a blank. Then I thought about Jesus. He never went to college. He never wrote a book and certainly was not a multi-millionaire. Jesus' impact on humanity has not been determined by all that He amassed in His life but by all He left behind. In Luke 22:28–29 He says, "You are those who have stood by me in my trials. And I confer on you a kingdom, just as my father conferred one on me." In other words, Jesus lived to leave a legacy. The ultimate yardstick of success is not measured by how much we have taken for ourselves in this life but by how much we have left behind for others when we go to the next.

Minute 3: Laughter

Zora Neale Hurston once commented, "I love myself when I am laughing."[2] As a person who wears a lot of hats—husband, father, brother, pastor, friend, and the list goes on—there is something about laughter that lightens my load and helps bring things back into perspective.

Psalm 2:4 states, "The One enthroned in heaven laughs." It goes on to explain that He laughs because of

His enemies. Why does God laugh? Because He knows that in the end His team will win. Real faith puts an expiration date on our moments of sorrow. Real faith learns to laugh at temporary setbacks, even at momentary shortcomings, because we know that in the end we are on the winning team. Let's not take ourselves so seriously! It may seem like your problem is going to get the last word; but the battle is the Lord's, and He is going to have the last laugh.

Chapter 2

MARRIAGE AND
FAMILY RELATIONSHIPS

Minute 4: Show People You Care

John Maxwell, an expert on gaining personal influence, states, "People do not care how much you know until they know how much you care."[1] In other words, before you attempt to direct, you must connect.

One day, my younger brother and I had a heated disagreement over the phone. After I got off the phone, my conscience was bothering me, and I defended myself, thinking, "I know I was right." Instantly, the Holy Spirit spoke to me, "You were right. But were you kind?" Sometimes winning the argument is not as important as maintaining a relationship. Proverbs 15:28 says, "The heart of the righteous weighs its answers." Think before you speak.

Minute 5: The "Ignorant Tool"

The other day, a friend and I put together a basketball hoop for my boys. About two hours into the ninety-degree evening, we reached for the hammer to make a part fit. It reminded me of when I was a kid. My father and I would try to fix something, and if we did not have the tools to fix it, Dad would say, "Son, hand me the ignorant tool." He would grab the hammer and beat the thing into submission.

This works with metal and wood but not so well in life. We tend to pound on people with bad language and name-calling because we do not have the right tools in our toolbox or have not developed the skill-set to use what we have properly. Ecclesiastes 10:10 says, "If the ax is dull and its edge unsharpened, more strength is needed but skill will bring success." It takes skill and grace to communicate, but it does not take much to be a hammer.

Minute 6: Marriage

When my wife and I were married, we were so in love. We expected the fairy tale, but instead it seemed like the beginning of a nuclear war. We were both convinced that God had us fall in love to punish us for sins future and past.

She did not live up to my expectations. I did not meet hers. I responded by constantly criticizing her, and she started to respond by nagging and withholding affection. The vicious cycle spun out of control until we realized a vital truth: we were in the same boat, and if we wanted to survive, we both needed to bail water.

It finally dawned on me that if she lost, I lost. She began to realize that my loss was her loss. We decided to make a minor adjustment. Instead of always trying to win, both of us began to make sure that the other person was always the winner. This little change caused our marriage to take on a strength that we could not have imagined. It was no longer about what I wanted from her but what I wanted for her, and vice versa.

This unlocked the practical power of 1 Corinthians 13: "[Love] is not self-seeking, it is not easily angered, it keeps no record of wrongs" (v. 5). We discovered that love is simply looking for the win-win formula in every situation.

Minute 7: Keep It Down

While I watched a famous mafia movie, I noticed that when life-and-death decisions were made, the godfather did not shout, jump up and down, or even turn red. He usually spoke just above a whisper. I have noticed that people who are really in charge do not have to go through a bunch of gyrations to get results. All they have to do is say the word.

In Matthew 8:8–9, a Roman soldier said to Jesus, "Lord, I do not deserve to have you come under my roof. But just say the word, and my servant will be healed. For I, myself, am a man under authority, with soldiers under me." In other words, the Roman soldier understood power. He didn't need to see a lightning flash or feel the ground shake. He just needed the word spoken from someone who had the authority. This truth really hit home when the Lord spoke to me after getting frustrated with my two children. He said, "If you have authority, you do not have to yell." Oops.

Minute 8: Leadership and Parenting

I am convinced that parenting in the modern world is the most rigorous leadership test any human can undergo. One of the biggest mistakes new parents make is thinking that their title equals power. By the time children become teenagers, parents begin to understand that only a track record of regard and earned respect can generate real influence in the lives of their children.

One of the best ways to measure if you are parenting well is to ask yourself, Do my children obey me because they have to or because they want to? Remember, they will only "have to" until they are eighteen. They will spend the rest of their lives living out their "want to's." We have to learn to do more than just spank the behind; we must also connect with the child's heart and mind. Proverbs 22:6 says, "Train a child in the way he should go, and when he is old he will not turn from it."

Minute 9: Insanity

A common definition of *insanity* is doing the same thing over and over again and expecting different results. Using this definition, most of us would have to admit that sometimes we are all a little bit crazy. We say the same things. We do the same things and go to the same places, yet somehow we expect things to change. But change doesn't happen until we do something new. Matthew 4:17 states, "Jesus began to preach, 'Repent for the kingdom of heaven is near.'" The term *repent* simply means "to change." Christ's message was summed up in one word, *change*.

In essence He was saying, "Those who do not embrace change cannot become my followers." So let's become a little more open to change. Instead of telling our loved ones about all the things they don't do, let's tell them how much we love and need them. Instead of fussing with that child, take him or her out for a pizza and remind yourself of the pleasure of sharing a good laugh. Maybe the people around you will change if you change first.

Minute 10: Mary

Matthew 1:18 says, "This is how the birth of Jesus came about: His mother Mary was pledged to be married to Joseph, but before they came together, she was found to be with child of the Holy Spirit."

I wonder why some people have so much trouble with this passage. If we can believe that God created the universe out of nothing and created Adam from the dirt, what is the stretch in believing that God would miraculously conceive Himself in a human womb? God is God, isn't He?

God was painstaking in making it clear in the biblical record that no male was involved in the

Incarnation. But when it came to raising Jesus, God absolutely refused to let Mary raise Him without a man to father Him. An angel appeared to Joseph in a dream and said, "Don't be afraid to take Mary home with you as your wife, for what is conceived in her is from the Holy Spirit" (Matt. 1:20). It takes both a male and female to accomplish the purposes of God in our children's lives. If Jesus needed a male role model, how much more do our children today? Perhaps you are not married to your child's father and can't think of one male that would be interested in mentoring your child, but remember, God still knows how to give men like Joseph dreams.

Minute 11: Not to Do List

The first thing I do when I get to my office in the morning is write my "things to do" list. It helps keep me on track for the day. However, as my responsibilities have grown, I have learned that I need not only create my "to do" list; I also create a "not to do" list.

This is also true at home.

- Item #1: Don't answer my wife too quickly when she talks to me. Listen first. Then speak.

- Item #2: Don't comment so much about petty things. Give my oldest son more space.

- Item #3: Stop eating so much junk food for lunch. How about eating more lunches that contain some broccoli, spinach, or cabbage?

This sounds really basic, but the concept has changed my life. Remember, all of the Ten Commandments begin with "Thou shalt not." So remember to balance your "things to do" list with a "things not to do" list. The results will amaze you.

Minute 12: Inventory

Once a year, warehouses shut down to take inventory so that they can find out the difference between what the accounting records say is in stock and what is actually on the shelves. Almost always, the warehouse has less than what is on paper. I have had times in my life that, like the business owner, I thought I had more on my shelves than I actually had. We tend to think that we are more kind, patient, and spiritual than we actually are. Second Corinthians 13:5 states, "Examine yourselves to see whether you are in the faith; test yourselves." In other words, take a personal inventory.

Sometimes we are not legends in our own time as much as legends in our own minds. At least once a year we should ask the people we love, Do I make you feel that you are valuable to me? Have I been patient with you? and so on. You might be surprised by the answers, but get over it and restock your shelves with what you need to be.

Minute 13: Dogs and Cans

I once heard a person on television tell a story about some mischievous boys and a stray dog. The boys had nothing to do, so they tied a string of cans around the dog's collar. The dog walked off at first, but the louder the dragging cans became, the faster he ran. Hours later, the boys found the dog motionless and exhausted, lying on a neighborhood lawn.

Often, we go from job to job, church to church, and relationship to relationship, not realizing that what we are running from is attached to us. Jesus said in Matthew 7:4–5, "How can you say to your brother, 'Let me take the speck out of your eye,' when all the time there is a plank in your own eye?...first take the plank out of your own eye, and then you will see clearly to remove the speck from your brother's eye." Before you point the finger at another's cans and cannots, make sure you have stopped running from your own.

Minute 14: Communication, Sex, and Money

Relationship experts say that communication, sex, and money are the three greatest areas of struggle in most relationships. But, like a tripod with only two legs, many people are out of balance because they somehow think that sex and money are outside their heavenly Father's purview.

You have heard it said, "What you do not know won't hurt you." Hosea 4:6 states, "My people are destroyed from lack of knowledge." The truth is, what you do not know is destroying you. No one can be expected to know more about a product than the manufacturer. If things are not working for you in your life, it is probably because you are not following the manufacturer's instruction manual. This Sunday around eleven o'clock in the morning, pull yourself into a shop and let a manufacturer's authorized dealer look under the hood. Remember, as with most products, if you do not use an authorized agent it will void the warranty. Get your oil change and let them replace your filters and fill you up with the fuel you need to be successful in life.

Minute 15: Success

One of the most important decisions you will make in your life is determining your definition of success. It is the internal measuring rod of our self-worth, level of personal satisfaction, and the guideline of all our dreams. How we characterize success is supremely important. Even the person who makes it his or her goal to be the most useless person in the world would have to decide what it means to be successfully useless.

In our world, success is often measured by the titles we hold and the things we obtain. When I turned forty, I had met most of my life's goals but still had a nagging feeling of failure. I had to do some soul-searching. I took a closer look at the life of Jesus for help. After He left His carpentry business, He lived on the charity of His followers. Isaiah 53:3 states that He was "despised and rejected of men." But today He is one of the most influential individuals who has ever lived. I discovered that true success is not always in the accolades or the size of the mountains we climb. Success is ultimately leaving behind much more than we take from the people we love.

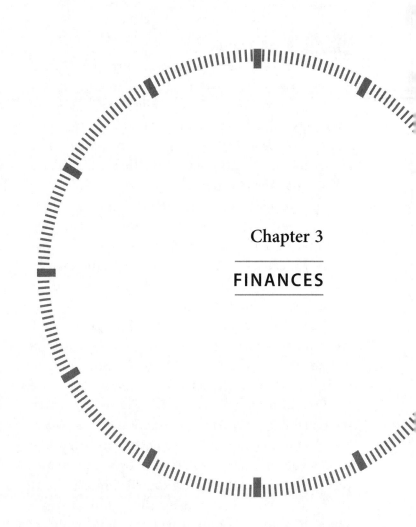

Chapter 3

FINANCES

Minute 16: 80/20 Rule

A fad spikes quickly but tends to turn down just as fast. A positive trend, on the other hand, has a slow but steady rise. Today, there is much teaching about prosperity using catchy slogans and novel ideas, but if we are wise, we will avoid the quick fixes and extremes and focus on establishing habits that will make a difference in the long term.

Years ago, I began to live by the 80/20 rule. I learned to first invest my tithe into God's economy and then invest the next 10 percent into my savings and investments. I made it a rule to live from no more than 80 percent of my income. This one decision has radically changed my financial destiny.

You might say, "I can't afford to do such a thing." The truth is you can't afford not to. If you live off 100 percent of your income, what are you going to do if something unexpected arises? When you give the first 10 percent to God, He promises to stretch the remaining 90 percent into more than you would have had if you kept 100 percent. When it comes to saving, you may need to start with only 1 percent of your income at first, but get started. Proverbs 13:11 states, "He who gathers money little by little makes it grow." If you are faithful, it will only be a matter of time before your money is working for you instead of you working for your money.

Minute 17: Bling

In Matthew 13:44, Jesus spoke this parable to teach his people about how to conduct business: "The kingdom of heaven is like treasure hidden in a field. When a man found it, he hid it again, and then in his joy he went and sold all he had and bought that field." Jesus was illustrating that sharp investors are always looking for undervalued purchases. Their motto is Buy Low and Sell High.

Most cars, clothing, and furniture are depreciating assets. We buy at high prices but have to sell them at low prices. On the other hand, an appreciating asset is something that gains value over time. The investor in the parable understood the value of obtaining an appreciating asset. He sold all his depreciating assets and invested the profits into the property that he secretly knew was undervalued. If we are going to be successful financially, it is important to learn that there is a big difference between looking prosperous and being prosperous. We may have to make some hard choices and postpone or even sell off a little bling so in the long run we can establish the real thing.

Minute 18: Management

Genesis teaches that when God created man, the first thing He did was put him in the Garden of Eden to manage it. God would not ask Adam to do something that he did not have the ability to do. Obviously innate in the makeup of mankind is the capacity to manage, and to do this well.

Much of life boils down to management. To have successful relationships, we must learn to manage conflict. If we are going to be successful on the job, we must learn to manage our priorities. What we manage well will grow, but whatever we mismanage, we will eventually lose. This is true with every area of life. Jesus says in Matthew 25:29, "Everyone who has will be given more, and he will have abundance. Whoever does not have, even what he has will be taken from him." Maybe our prayer should not be for God to give us more but to learn to manage what we already have, better.

Minute 19: God and Money

Jesus said, "You cannot serve both God and money" (Matt. 6:24). Notice that He did not say that you cannot love God and have money. He warned against loving money and still trying to pretend that you worship God.

True worship has little to do with church buildings and liturgies. Worship is really about priorities. Jesus said to His followers, "Seek first his kingdom and his righteousness, and all these things will be given to you as well" (Matt. 6:33).

If you think about it, the thing that makes God truly

God is not the fact that He is holy, loving, and righteous, although we are thankful for these attributes. It is the fact that He was first. Whatever we seek first in our lives has the ultimate position. God understands this and takes us through seasons in which we must make hard financial choices about what we will make our priority. Through this process He proves the genuineness of our faith. Always remember, where your treasure is your heart will be also. God does not need our money, but He does require our heart.

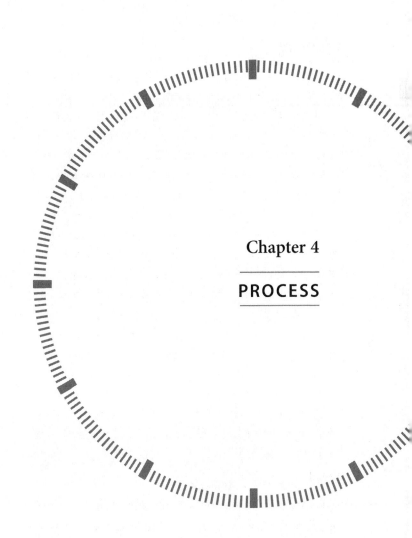

Chapter 4

PROCESS

Minute 20: Rats

A friend of mine once told me about a scientist who wanted to prove the power of hope. He put rats in a dish of water with sides too high to climb and water too deep to stand in. The rats could only swim. However, after a few minutes, the rats stopped swimming and drowned. A scientist decided to remove one of the rats from the dish when it stopped swimming (but before it actually drowned), and later subjected it to the same experiment with a fresh set of rats. He found that the rat did not drown in a few minutes like the rest, but it swam for more than twenty-four hours. What transformed this rat? The fact that it had been saved before gave it hope that it would happen again.

Sometimes God delivers us after only minutes, and other times deliverance comes in days or years. Why? Is it because He loses His love for us or because He is the God who understands the necessity of building the spiritual muscle called hope? Romans 15:13 says, "May the God of hope fill you with all joy and peace as you trust in him."

Minute 21: What Is Peace?

The ancient philosopher Seneca made the observation, "The mind is never right but when it is at peace within itself."[1]

But what is peace? It is the ability to stay in one

piece when pressure tempts you to fall apart. Peace is having an inward grip on heaven when you are going through what feels like hell.

Ultimately, peace is like having a Seeing Eye dog. It comes from a heart that has learned to trust even when it cannot see. Jesus said, "Peace I leave with you; My peace I give you. I do not give to you as the world gives" (John 14:27). The mind is never really right, but when we learn to trust God.

Minute 22: Working Your Rock

There was a sickly unemployed man that was a month behind in his mortgage. He looked out his front door and found that a two-ton rock had fallen out of the sky onto his lawn. He did not have the money to have it hauled away, so every morning he chiseled the rock with a hammer and wheeled it into his backyard.

After a week his skin was bronzed. The second week he was able to work on the rock for hours at a time. By the end of the month his health came back. By the end of the second month his muscles were ripped and he was ready to take on the world again. A neighbor stopped by who happened to own a rock quarry and offered him fifty cents a pound for the rock chips, as well as a job. The money was enough to catch up on his mortgage with a little left over.

Romans 8:28 says, "God causes all things to work

together for good to those who love God" (NAS). But God does not work for those who will not work for themselves.

Minute 23: Failure and Success

Failure is a vital part of success. If you never failed, you have probably never tried anything of value. The great basketball icon Michael Jordan said, "I've missed more than nine thousand shots in my career. I've lost almost three hundred games. Twenty-six times, I've been trusted to take the game-winning shot and missed. I've failed over and over and over again in my life. And that is why I succeed."[2]

One day, Jesus turned and looked at one of His disciples and said, "Simon, Simon, Satan has asked to sift you as wheat, but I have prayed for you, Simon, that your faith may not fail" (Luke 22:31–32). Simon responded by saying that he would never betray Jesus, but hours later he did just that. Most would expect God to have given up on such a wishy-washy disciple, but He is not looking for people who have never failed. Instead He is looking for people who refuse to stay down after they have been knocked down. Failure only becomes fatal when you believe that you cannot get back up again.

Minute 24: **Grass Is Always Greener**

You have heard the expression that the grass is always greener on the other side. The reason the grass is so green is because the people on the other side have had to walk through a bunch of cow dung. If you want to accomplish anything of value, you are going to have to go through some troubles. No one arrives at the top without a story to tell.

If you let the manure do its fertilizing, it won't be long before what was intended for evil begins to work for your good. In the end it will develop a strength that will make you vibrant and strong. Proverbs 14:4 states, "Where no oxen are, the manger is clean" (NAS). Remember, the ox was the largest work animal in the near East. The point is, the only time there are no piles of mess, when "the manger is clean," is when nothing is getting done. If you want to make any progress, you are going to have to get used to using a shovel. Remember the words of Frederick Douglass: "If there is no struggle, there is no progress."[3]

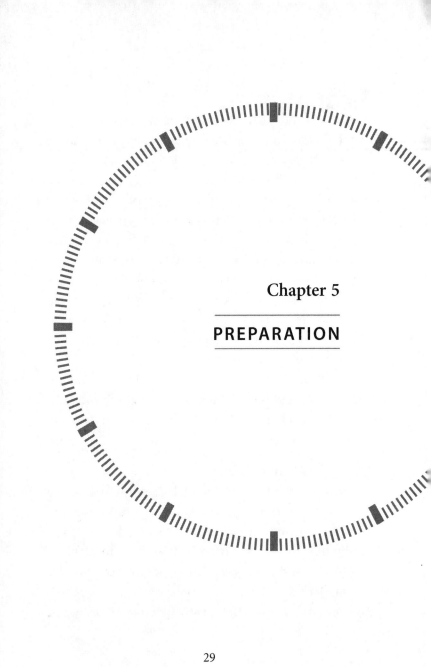

Chapter 5

PREPARATION

Minute 25: No "I"

The natural progression of things is that we are taught before we teach, we rent before we own, and we live under our parents' rules before we can make our own. Jesus said in Luke 16:12, "If you have not been trustworthy with someone else's property, who will give you property of your own?" The greatest test of character is not how well we advance our own interests but how willing we are to advance the interests of others. If we learn to make others look good, become agreeable to someone else's way of doing things, or help someone else fulfill his or her vision, we will discover that whatever we make happen for others, God will make happen for us.

Sometimes promotions are withheld not because of our aptitude but our attitude. There is no *I* in the word *team*. Get over yourself and you might get on faster in your career.

Minute 26: Complacency

Seafarers say that the most dangerous time at sea is when the waters are calm. When the sun is out and the ocean is smooth, sailors tend to walk further from the railing and are less careful about their footing.

Storms on the seas are often sudden, and if you are not vigilant at all times, you could very easily be tossed overboard. Likewise, the most dangerous times in our lives are not in the middle of a storm but typically right after our victories. In these moments, we tend to bask in the glory of our most recent achievement and start to let our guards down. First Corinthians 10:12 states, "If you think you are standing firm, be careful that you don't fall!" Are you still holding on tightly to God, or have you become a little overconfident? If yesterday's achievements have become your finish line, you too are finished. Stay connected, stay ready, and always be fired up about the possibilities ahead.

Minute 27: Coach

The other day, I tried to teach my son to improve his jump shot. I showed him that a jump shot had to be taken with his wrists above his head if he was going to use his height advantage; then, I went inside the house. One half hour later, my son came into the house mad because he was not able to make the shot using the new form. In my typical Dad manner, I said, "OK, then let people keep blocking your shot."

I am not a professional basketball player, but I am sure that I know enough to help a fifth-grader play better. James 1:21 says, "Humbly accept the word planted in you, which can save you." If we do not learn to receive training from those with a little more experience, we will keep having our shots blocked in life. If we want to succeed, we must remain coachable. The power to learn is directly affected by our willingness to accept advice.

Minute 28: Seasons

Abraham Lincoln said, "If I had eight hours to chop down a tree, I'd spend six hours sharpening my ax."[1] Jesus spent thirty years of His life preparing for only three years of ministry. Sometimes, we are in such a hurry that we forget what goes up fast, usually comes down fast.

Before you make another New Year's resolution, let's consider the words of Solomon, "There is a time for everything...a time to be born and a time to die, a time to plant and a time to uproot, a time to kill and a time to heal, a time to tear down and a time to build, a time to weep and a time to laugh, a time to mourn and a time to dance...a time to search and a time to give up, a time to keep and a time to throw away, a time to tear and a time to mend, a time to be silent and a time to speak" (Eccles. 1–4, 6–7). Let's not try to have a harvest when it is our season to plant. Knowing which season you are in, in your life might spare you a lot of heartache and disappointment.

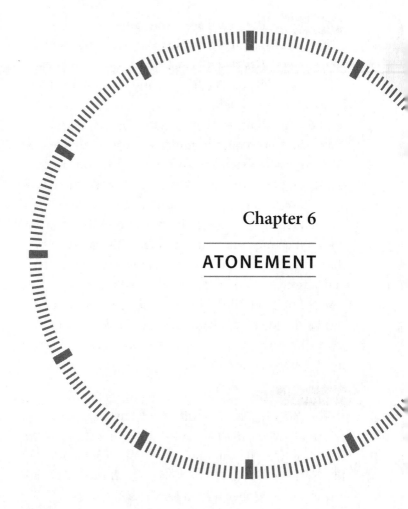

Chapter 6

ATONEMENT

Minute 29: The Ten Commandments

A man cheated on his taxes and was caught by the government. His defense was, "Everyone else does it, so why should I be fined?" Not only was he fined, but he was also put in jail.

The Ten Commandments state: Thou shall not lie. Thou shall not commit adultery. Thou shall not lust after your neighbor's house or spouse, and the list goes on. If you have ever lied, cheated, or lusted, in the eyes of the law you are a liar, a cheater, and a pervert.

The fact that everyone else has also broken the law does not change the commandment. The good news is that if we throw ourselves on the mercy of the court and admit our missteps, Jesus is willing to take our case before God. First Timothy 2:5 states, "For there is one God and one mediator between God and men, the man Christ Jesus." Jesus has never lost a case. But you must confess before He can bless.

Minute 30: Bell Tower

The British had a tradition of hanging convicted criminals when the bell tolled at eight o'clock in the morning. One day, a convicted felon was escorted to the platform. A white hood was placed over his head, and the executioner waited for the bell to ring.

At eight o'clock, the bell rope was pulled, but there was no sound. It was pulled again and then again.

Soon, droplets of blood dripped from the bell onto the man who pulled the rope. He looked up to see what was happening and saw that a man had wrapped his body around the fifty-pound gong of the bell and had kept the bell from ringing.

The convicted man's younger brother had climbed the bell tower to keep the bell from tolling. The executioner and the crowd were silenced by the sight. They decided that one death was enough for the day and allowed the convicted man to go free. Jesus has climbed your bell tower. John 8:36 says, "If the Son sets you free, you will be free indeed."

Minute 31: The Measure of a King

The English needed to standardize their units of measurement. They decided to determine the length of a yard by measuring the distance between King Henry I's nose and thumb.

Today, many are saying, "I do not need all that Jesus stuff." After all, I am not as bad as the next guy. Paul comments, "When we measure ourselves by ourselves and compare ourselves with ourselves, we are not wise." (See 2 Corinthians 10:12.) When we compare our faults with those of other mortals, we tend to walk away feeling justified. However, if Jesus is the immortal King, His life should be the ultimate standard of measurement. The question is not, How do you line up against your neighbor? but, How well have you aligned yourself with Christ? The statement "Jesus is Lord" is more than a catch phrase. It is a statement demonstrated in our lifestyle and measured by the length of our willingness to obey.

Minute 32: The Great Exchange

Have you ever handed a cashier a ten-dollar bill, only to be given change as if you had given just a dollar? Did you complain? If they refused to correct the situation, did you promise never to go back to that store?

Following Christ has been called the great exchange. We meet God at the cross and exchange our faults for His mercy. But the requirement is simple—all of us, for all of Him. Sometimes we try to shortchange God and wonder why He seems so distant. Jeremiah 29:13 states, "You will seek me and find me when you seek me with all your heart." If you want to be successful in your walk with God, it is an all-or-nothing proposition.

Minute 33: The Naked Truth

Before I became a believer, I spent hours studying the world's major religions and philosophies in the hope of finding the truth. Christian friends told me that I did not need to understand the Bible, only believe it. I was relieved when I discovered that the Bible taught otherwise. First Peter 3:15 says, "Always be prepared to give an answer to everyone who asks you to give the reason for the hope that you have." It wasn't until someone was prepared to explain the Scriptures to me that I could believe them.

I heard this story around that time in my life: One day Truth undressed to go swimming. While Truth was swimming, Lie stole his clothes. Then Lie put on Truth's clothes and visited the nearest town. For hours, Lie masqueraded as Truth until, eventually, the sheriff told his deputy to arrest Lie. The townspeople said, "Why should we arrest that man?" The sheriff said, "Because I can see the naked Truth running up the hill."

Sometimes people are confused, not because they do not want to believe but because no one has had the patience to point out the naked Truth.

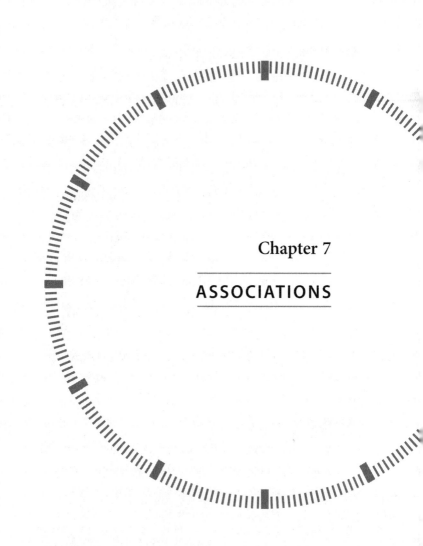

Chapter 7

ASSOCIATIONS

Minute 34: A Lesson from Geese

I do not need a prophetic gift to predict where you will be in five years. Anyone can forecast your tomorrow by looking at the people you hang around today. First Corinthians 15:33 says, "Do not be misled: 'Bad company corrupts good character.'" Imagine what good company might do!

Many people have questioned the importance of becoming part of a church. I think the answer can be illustrated in nature. I have read that when geese form the V formation, the whole flock adds over 70 percent to its flying range. When each bird flaps its wings, it becomes uplift for the birds that are following.

Please don't mishear me. Don't just join any church, but find a church where you experience uplift. Find a church that flies in divine order, and then don't just sit and stare; connect your gifts and talents to the formation.

Minute 35: The Ministry

When the subject of preachers comes up at the Thanksgiving table, watch out. At least one member of the family is going to have a personal experience with abuse while the rest are going to give examples of a preacher having a house that is too big or a car that is too expensive. Often the criticism is well deserved, but what concerns me is the idea that ministers are held to a higher standard than others. This idea is dangerous. There is only one standard for all men. Ministers don't read a different Bible.

James 3 states, "Not many of you should presume to be teachers, my brothers, because you know that we who teach will be judged more strictly." Preachers do not have a different standard but a stricter judgment based on the same standard. The next time you criticize the clergy, make sure you are holding him or her to the same standard as you would yourself and let God judge anything beyond that.

Minute 36: Adam and Eve

Right after Adam and Eve ate from the tree of the knowledge of good and evil in Genesis 3:9, the Lord called to the man and said, "Where are you?" Is it that God did not know where Adam was? God asked the question not because he could not find Adam but to help Adam find himself.

Everyone needs at least one person in his or her life who is allowed to ask the hard questions. Where are you now? Are you hiding behind mistakes or facing them? Are you shifting responsibility and making your past another excuse for why you no longer try? Instead of the Lord having to hunt you down and ask, "Where are you?" why not take the initiative and say, "Lord, here I am, faults, blemishes, and all. I have no excuses and no one else to blame. All I ask for is Your mercy and grace to do better." This is a very simple prayer, but it often gets profound results.

Minute 37: Friends and Chickens

Jesus said to a group of fishermen, "Come follow me and I will make you fishers of men" (Mark 1:17). The promise was simple; if they followed, Jesus would make them fishers of men. The law of association states that you will become like the top three people you know. In other words, if you want to know where you are going to end up in life, take a look at your closest associates.

This law so affected Christ's disciples that Acts 4:13 states, "When they saw the courage of Peter and John and realized that they were unschooled, ordinary men, they were astonished and they took note that these men had been with Jesus." Over time, Jesus had rubbed off on them. The term *anointing* is really not very mysterious; all it means is "rubbed-on oil." If you want to increase the anointing in your life, you just need to upgrade those you rub shoulders with. You will never soar like an eagle if you continue pecking with chickens.

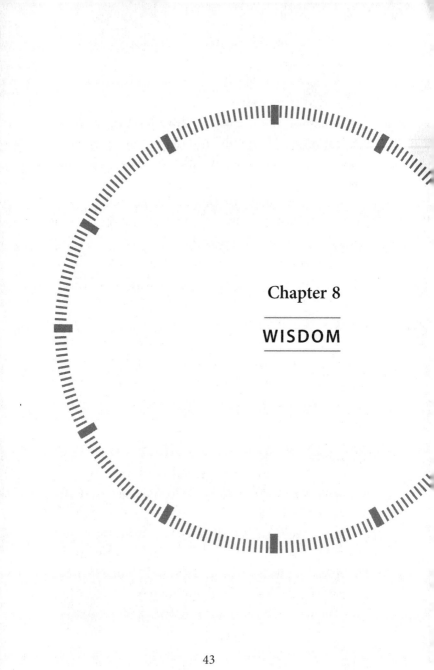

Chapter 8

WISDOM

Minute 38: Get a Grip

Have you ever picked up a steaming hot coffee cup without using the handle? Man, it burns. Handles are designed to help diffuse the heat so we can safely pick up a hot cup.

Sometimes situations in life get heated, but God has provided us with handles to keep us from getting burned. Proverbs 15:1 is one such handle: "A gentle answer turns away wrath, but a harsh word stirs up anger."

Have you ever noticed that it takes two to fight? My wife learned this years ago. When I would get angry, she would respond by being sweet. She understood that I could not have an argument by myself. The next time someone goes off on you, pause and get a grip. Remember you can catch more flies with honey than vinegar.

Minute 39: The Power of the Tongue

Years ago, something painful happened to me. It was totally unexpected and I was deeply wounded. No matter what I did, I could not get the thing off my mind. And the more I talked about it, the more it seemed to fester. Proverbs 18:21 states, "The tongue has the power of life and death." I did not realize that each time I put the situation in my mouth, I was peeling back the scab and only delaying the healing process.

I have since learned that after I talk through or pray through a matter, I need to be quiet about it. I do not add logs to a fire that I wish would burn out. You can have life or death by what you choose to talk about, or what you choose to stop talking about. The power is yours.

Minute 40: Get Understanding

Helen Keller said of Philippians 4:7, "I do not want the peace which passeth understanding, I want the understanding which bringeth peace."[1] She misunderstood the scripture, but she was on to something. Solomon says, "Though it cost all you have, get understanding" (Prov. 4:7). I often hear people say, "I have done all I know to do, but nothing seems to work." But that statement belies the problem. You may have done all you know to do; the problem is sometimes that we just do not know enough.

I have experienced life-altering miracles from God, and I am very grateful. But I have also found that if I operate with greater understanding, I will not need as many miracles. Before we ask God for our next miracle, maybe we should ask Him to give us greater wisdom about how we should conduct our affairs. In large measure, miracles are God's way of correcting things that have already gone wrong. But if we pursue wisdom, we can often intercept problems before they even happen.

Minute 41: Halt

Years ago, I received advice from a veteran of the faith who has kept me anchored through very rough moments. He said, "Whenever you are confronted by trying circumstances, remember the acronym HALT. If you are 'hungry, angry, lonely, or tired,' apply the twenty-four hour rule."

I have learned that in such times it is wise to give myself twenty-four hours to gain perspective. If I do this, it gives me a chance not to speak out of my hurt but that which is best for the situation. Ephesians 4:29 says, "Do not let any unwholesome talk come out of your mouths, but only what is helpful for building others up according to their needs, that it may benefit those who listen."

When we are hungry, angry, lonely, or tired, our personal condition often causes us to see our concerns as primary and the needs of others as secondary. According to Ephesians, we should not respond to only benefit ourselves, but our first concern must be the benefit of the listener. Often, a delayed response is better than a bad one.

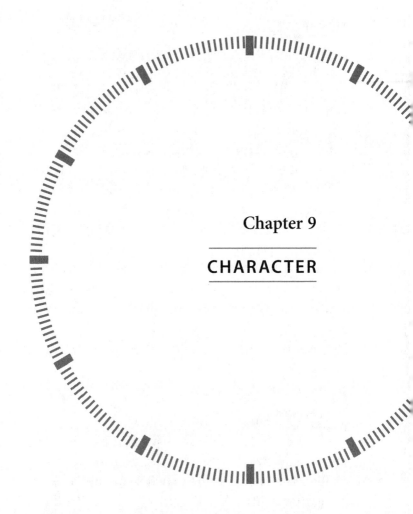

Chapter 9

CHARACTER

Minute 42: Guard Your Heart

It does not take a lot of skill to tear down a fence, but it takes a lot of hard work to put one up. If you are going to attempt something worthwhile in life, it is important to learn to tune certain people out. The first thing I do whenever I am criticized is to consider the source. Is the critic qualified? Have they ever been in my situation before? Then I rule out certain critiques.

The second thing I try to do is understand their motive. Do they care about me? It is not a good investment of my emotions to lose sleep thinking about the opinions of people who would not cry at my funeral.

Lastly, I have to guard against becoming so offended that I cannot look for the kernel of truth. Criticism is always an opportunity to grow. So keep your heart and words sweet, because if your critic is right, you may have to eat them. Proverbs 4:23 states, "Above all else, guard your heart." If you don't guard your heart, no one else will.

Minute 43: Keeping Myself Honest

I had a jogging buddy who was on a diet. I was not very supportive, because he had been on a diet for as long as I knew him. For a whole month, he would congratulate himself for eating three small meals a day, even though I could see his shorts getting tighter. At the end of the month, he asked me to get out my scale so he could weigh himself. He was ten pounds heavier. He was devastated. It is one thing to twist the truth for others, but it is far more painful when you lie to yourself.

We are all tempted to tell less than the truth at times. R. T. Kendall says, "A lie is merely the postponement of a truth that is eventually going to come out."[1] In Matthew 10:26, Jesus said it this way, "There is nothing concealed that will not be disclosed, or hidden that will not be made known." In other words, what we do in secret will be brought into the light. So why cause further embarrassment by postponing the inevitable? You can just say it or delay it. But the truth will eventually come out.

Minute 44: What Do Your Clothes Smell Like?

I am not proud of this, but when I was a kid I had my share of fistfights. Even the times I won, I was left with cuts and bruises that took time to heal.

Second Corinthians 2:14 says, "Thanks be to God who always leads us in triumph in Christ" (NAS). God promises us that we will win, but sometimes it is not without a fight. In Acts 14, Paul was stoned. God prevailed, and His servant miraculously survived; but after the broken teeth, crushed bones, and the holes that the stones left in his face, he needed not only to survive but also to be healed.

You may have survived another week, but have you

been healed? The Book of Daniel tells us about three Hebrew boys who were thrown into the fire for obeying God but miraculously came out without the smell of smoke on their clothes. They not only survived, but they did so without the smell of bitterness, unforgiveness, or disgrace on their wardrobe. You may have survived, but what would people who are closest to you say your closet smells like?

Minute 45: Big Little *U* in Ministry

One day I was complaining to God about a situation that was difficult for me. After a great deal of patience, He responded, "The only thing I hurt was your pride." The letter *I* is conveniently placed in the middle of the word *pride*. Sometimes we let our *I*'s become the center of lives.

Philippians 2:3 says, "Do nothing out of selfish ambition or vain conceit, but in humility consider others better than yourselves." We cannot defeat the big *I* until we look at our loved ones and decide our first concern is *U*. It may not please an English teacher to write lowercase *i*'s and capital *U*'s in an essay, but it would surely please God if we so punctuated our hearts.

Minute 46: Humility

Everything of value is imitated. It may look like the original, sound like the original, even smell like the original; but after closer inspection, we discover that it is not what we had hoped. The same is true with ideals.

I desperately wanted to be godly, so I naturally wanted to be humble. I did everything I could not to stand out. I would dumb down, dress down, and speak down—anything it took to fit in with those I wanted to be down with. Then I read a quote from St. Paul: "Do not let anyone who delights in false [pseudo] humility and the worship of angels disqualify you for the prize" (Col. 2:18). Paul was saying that if ever we bow down to anything less than ourselves, we are not being humble but disqualifying ourselves from the prize. I realized that even humility has a counterfeit.

Never subtract from whom God has created you to be, to be down with a crowd. True humility not only recognizes our weaknesses but also acknowledges our strengths.

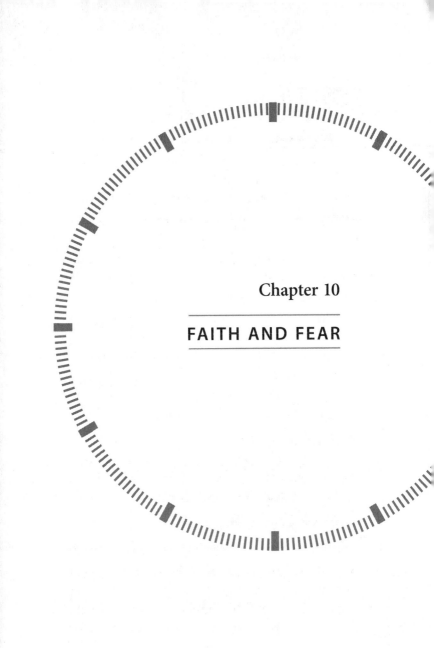

Chapter 10

FAITH AND FEAR

Minute 47: Do Not Be Afraid

A scholar once stated that "Do not be afraid" appears 365 times in the Bible, once for every day of the year. Although I've never counted for myself, I can imagine this is true. A common acronym for the word *fear* is "false evidence appearing real." We usually become afraid when we confuse facts (false evidence) with the truth.

The fact may be that you are having some troubles in your relationships, but the biblical truth is, "Love never fails" (1 Cor. 13:8).

The fact may be that you are sinking in debt, but the truth is, "If any of you lacks wisdom, let him ask of God, who gives to all liberally and without reproach" (James 1:5, NKJV).

The fact may be that you feel like giving up, but the truth is, "Having done everything to stand, stand firm" (Eph. 6:13, NAS).

Facts are only as big as our faith allows them to be. Faith is often sticking with the truth until it gets so big in our hearts that even the facts have to say "amen."

Minute 48: Timothy

Young Timothy was frightened. With every footstep he heard outside his door, he thought it might be Roman soldiers coming to arrest him. The persecution of the church under Emperor Nero had reached a fever pitch, and Timothy started to give out under the weight of it all.

Meanwhile, the apostle Paul, imprisoned in a cold dungeon awaiting his execution, wrote these life-changing words to Timothy: "God has not given us a spirit of fear, but a spirit of power and of love and of a sound mind" (2 Tim. 1:7, NKJV).

You might have expected Paul to be more sympathetic, but this was not what the young pastor really needed. Timothy needed to man up, square his shoulders, lift up his head, and know where his hope came from. Like you, I have had many days when I have felt like finding a corner somewhere to crawl into and hide. But Scripture tells us that God did not give us that quitting, shrinking, running away spirit; but inexplicable inner strength, pure vision, and the ability to keep our head in the worst of situations. What God gives you, let no one take away.

Minute 49: Seed

In 2005, scientists germinated a seed excavated from Herod the Great's palace in Israel. Although the seed was two thousand years old, it grew into a three-foot-tall plant.

Jesus taught, "The kingdom of heaven is like a...seed" (Matt. 13:31). A seed is something that holds tremendous potential but cannot grow until it is planted. Many people think that the message of God's kingdom is outdated, but just like King Herod's seed, if it gets planted in the heart, it has the same potential for miracles as it did two thousand years ago. After all, as Hebrews 13:8 says, "Jesus is the same yesterday and today and forever."

In my early thirties, I suffered from a debilitating disease. After five surgeries, the doctors had given up and I was left with constant bleeding and excruciating pain. I had prayed for years with no success, until one day, after a time of prayer, I knew something in me was different. I returned to the doctor days later, and the doctor verified that I was completely healed. There was no natural explanation for the events except that Jesus, who healed the sick two thousand years ago, still heals today. His Word is like a seed; if you get it into your heart, it will grow.

Minute 50: Conspiracy Theory

How many of us have heard that NASA faked the moon landing or that our government was behind the events of 9/11? We still hear of Elvis sightings. A conspiracy theory is basically the belief that behind a major event is a deceptive plot by a secret and powerful group to advance their agenda.

Many theories are false, but sometimes they do happen. As a person who has spent some time on Capitol Hill, I understand that there is always a story behind the story. Jeremiah 29:11 states, "'For I know the plans I have for you,' declares the LORD, 'plans to prosper you and not to harm you, plans to give you hope and a future.'" According to Jeremiah, not only are our enemies conspiring, but so is God. He is ever planning and scheming for our good. The next time you are in a crisis, realize that the conspiracy to bless you is so much greater than the conspiracy to do you harm. Keep your head up.

Minute 51: More Faith

I think the best description of the word *faith* is "trust." Trust is the quiet assurance that comes from knowing that a person or a thing will do what you expect. Paul says in 2 Thessalonians 1:3, "We ought always to thank God for you, brothers, and rightly so, because your faith is growing more and more." How does faith grow? Trust, like faith, grows only with time and experience.

Faith usually comes from interacting with people and discovering what we can expect from them. Because I spend so much time with my wife, when I pull into my driveway I usually know what to expect. The same is true with God. The more time I invest in His presence, the easier it is for me to know what to expect. Sometimes we do not believe as we should, not because God is so hard to trust, but because we have invested so little time. God plus an open heart and time spent with Him equals more faith.

Minute 52: A Turtle's Faith

This morning I stepped off of my front porch and almost put two hundred pounds and my hard-surfaced dress shoes on the back of a foot-long turtle. The turtle was as surprised as I was, but all he did was stick his neck back into his shell.

How could it be so calm? The turtle was at peace with the fact that it was not born with the speed to outrun trouble. Instead, it was given armor to withstand it. Psalm 119:114 states, "You are my refuge and my shield; I have put my hope in your word." Sometimes the greatest expression of faith is when we withdraw into the shell of the Word of God and just trust. I have seen a turtle walk away from a one hundred-pound biting dog simply because it had the good sense to trust its shell. Has God provided more for turtles than you and me? Ephesians 6:13 says, "Therefore put on the full armor of God, so that when the day of evil comes, you may be able to stand your ground."

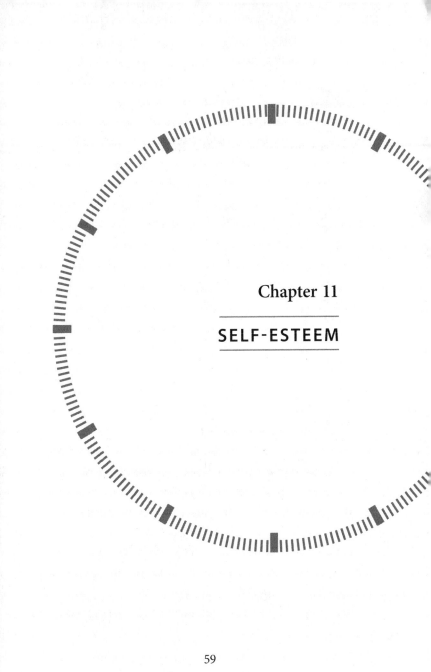

Chapter 11

SELF-ESTEEM

Minute 53: What You Put Up With

Frederick Douglass offered some advice that has been a guide for me: "Power concedes nothing without a demand. It never did and it never will. Find out just what any people will quietly submit to and you have found out the exact amount of injustice and wrong which will be imposed upon them…The limits of tyrants are prescribed by the endurance of those whom they oppress."[1] In other words, no one can ride your back unless you bend over. So, stop complaining about those who are trying to ride you and stand up. Jesus said in Matthew 16:19, "Whatever you permit on earth is permitted in heaven and whatever you forbid on earth is forbidden in heaven." Maybe your problem is not so much what a certain person is trying to do to you but what you are willing to put up with.

Minute 54: The Enemy Within

An African proverb states, "If there is no enemy within, there is no enemy without." Jesus did not talk much about the devil's operations outside of people hearts. Why did Jesus not teach more on the subject? As long as Satan is on the outside of a person, he is not much of a threat. It is only when he enters our hearts through word, thought, or deed that he gains real power and control.

Satan tries everything in his power to stop God's

plan for our lives, but as long as his work is external, we have no reason to fear. Romans 8:38–39 exudes with this confidence: "For I am convinced that neither death nor life, neither angels nor demons, neither the present nor the future, nor any powers, neither height nor depth, nor anything else in all creation, will be able to separate us from the love of God that is in Christ Jesus our Lord." We have nothing to fear but fear itself.

Minute 55: Nothing to Prove

God's introduction of Himself in Scripture does not begin with any explanations or justifications. Genesis 1:1 simply states, "In the beginning God...." As the song title says, "Whoomp! There it is!" Later, Moses is at the burning bush and asks God, "What is your name?" God's response is short: "I AM WHO I AM" (Exod. 3:14). In the New Testament, some people were arguing with Jesus about His identity, and Jesus settled it with one statement: "Most assuredly, I say to you, before Abraham was, I AM" (John 8:58).

People may try to saddle you with arguments against who you are, where you came from, or what you can ultimately do. But you will never experience true freedom until you decide that you have nothing to prove. I am, because God chose me to be. God gives us friends to hold us accountable, but I should never have to explain to establish my value.

Minute 56: The Lion

This story was once told to me by my friend Dr. Myles Munroe:[2]

> Once a shepherd adopted a lost lion cub and let the lion join his flock of sheep. The lion learned to eat grass and even *baa* like the sheep. One day, the herd became agitated and started to panic. The lion asked, "Why is everyone so frightened?" The sheep told him that a vicious beast was just over the hill.
>
> The cub peeked over the hill and saw the most frightening beast he had ever seen. The beast released the fiercest roar that the cub had ever heard. He was terrified and ran back to the safety of the herd, trembling.
>
> Months later, he went to drink at that same stream. As he drank he saw the reflection of the beast. He let out the loudest scream he could, but what came out his mouth was a roar like the beast. It was scary, but it felt so good. Full of adrenaline, his muscles tightened and a confidence overcame him as he dared to go back to the water's edge to look again at the beast in the water. As he looked, the beast mirrored his every movement, and he realized for the first time that he was not a sheep but a lion.

Many of us are *baa*-ing through life, when God has created us to roar. Proverbs 28:1 says, "But the righteous are as bold as a lion."

Chapter 12

A SPIRIT OF EXCELLENCE

Minute 57: A Two-Mile Culture

Culture has been defined as the shared patterns of thought and behavior, relationships, and understanding that are learned through socialization. What would the world be like if religious people spent less time focusing on the debatable portions of Scripture and created a counterculture that practiced just a few of the teachings that are crystal clear? Let's experiment for a moment and ignore every statement Jesus made, except one: "If someone forces you to go one mile, go with him two miles" (Matt. 5:41).

Imagine workplaces where everyone does more than required. Imagine homes where every family member gives to the next more than they deserve. Imagine marriages where the most pressing question in the relationship is not, How can I get more? but, What more can I give? Maybe I am a dreamer, but imagine what the world would be like if Christians really began to follow Christ.

Minute 58: Bring Simple Back

The key to healthy relationships is simple—love others as yourself. The key to weight loss is simple—move more and eat better. The key to creating wealth is equally simple—invest wisely and waste less. Life can be simple, but sometimes doing the right thing can be hard.

Paul says in Romans 7:21, "When I want to do good, evil is right there with me." He goes on to say, "Who will rescue me from this body of death?" (v. 24). He was saying that sometimes his walk with God made him feel like he was buried with a corpse in a casket and he was slowly running out of air. This was a terribly painful situation. But Paul ends this crisis by saying, "Thanks be to God—through Jesus Christ our Lord" (v. 25). In the midst of his trial, he released the solution and gave thanks and praise. If you praise Him while in distress, He will raise you out of the test. No matter how low you have sunk, if you begin to thank God in the middle of your funk, God will give you the grace to slam dunk in the middle of all the junk.

Minute 59: The Power of Focus and Forgetting

Some time ago, I did some martial arts training with my son. When it came to breaking boards, I was a little intimidated. But the instructor trained us to mentally see our hands go to a point beyond the wood, before we struck. We were to use all of our strength to move our hands to that point. On my first try, I broke a board that I would never have imagined that I could break.

The apostle Paul understood this power of focus. In Philippians 3:13–14 he said, "But one thing I do: Forgetting what is behind and straining toward what is ahead, I press on toward the goal to win the prize."

Focus and forgetting are two sides of the same coin. To focus, we have to filter out the extraneous and zoom in to the vital. Who we used to be becomes irrelevant, if we get a big enough vision of who God is making us. This journey really begins in the heart. We have to see ourselves where we want to be, before we are ready to go.

Minute 60: Excellence

Actor Michael J. Fox made this statement, "I am careful not to confuse excellence with perfection. Excellence, I can reach for; perfection is God's business."[1] The most anyone can ever do in life is his or her very best. Sometimes we find that our best is not enough and in such moments all that we can do is trust God.

The King James Version of the Bible says in Psalm 138:8, "The LORD will perfect that which concerneth me." I do not know what Michael J. Fox believes about God, but he stated a biblical truth. All of us must make peace with the fact that we are less than perfect. But we must daily wage war against any notion that we should settle for being anything less than excellent.

NOTES

Chapter 1
HAPPINESS

1. Abraham Lincoln quote available at http://www
.brainyquote.com/quotes/quotes/a/abrahamlin100845.html
(accessed 1/7/09).

2. Zora Neale Hurston quote available at http://www
.goodreads.com/author/quotes/15151.Zora_Neale_Hurston
(accessed 1/7/09).

Chapter 2
MARRIAGE AND FAMILY RELATIONSHIPS

1. John Maxwell quote available at http://thinkexist.com/
quotation/people_do_not_care_how_much_you_know_
until_they/346868.html (accessed 1/7/09).

Chapter 4
PROCESS

1. Seneca quote available at http://thinkexist.com/quotes/
with/keyword/in_his_right_mind/ (accessed 1/8/09).

2. Michael Jordan quote available at http://www
.brainyquote.com/quotes/authors/m/michael_jordan.html
(accessed 1/8/09).

3. Frederick Douglass quote available at http://thinkexist
.com/quotation/if_there_is_no_struggle-there_is_no_
progress/206199.html (accessed 1/8/09).

Chapter 5
PREPARATION

1. Abraham Lincoln quote available at http://thinkexist
.com/quotation/if_i_had_eight_hours_to_chop_down_a_
tree-i-d/194268.html (accessed 1/8/09).

Chapter 8
WISDOM

1. Helen Keller quote available at http://www.brainyquote
.com/quotes/authors/h/helen_keller.html (accessed 1/8/09).

Chapter 9
CHARACTER

1. R. T. Kendall, *Controlling the Tongue* (Lake Mary, FL:
Charisma House, 2007), 115.

Chapter 11
SELF-ESTEEM

1. Frederick Douglass quote available at "About Us," We
the People, http://www.givemeliberty.org/aboutus.htm
(accessed 1/21/09).

2. Dr. Myles Munroe, from his address at the 2006
International Third World Leaders Association Conference.

Chapter 12
A SPIRIT OF EXCELLENCE

1. Michael J. Fox quote available at http://www.brainyquote
.com/quotes/authors/m/michael_j_fox.html (accessed 1/9/09).

ABOUT THE AUTHOR

D R. GRIER HELD HIS FIRST PASTORATE IN a small storefront church among the prostitutes and homeless in a drug-infested area of Washington, DC. He often comments that this is where he really attended seminary. In 1998, Dr. Grier established Grace Church. The church is located in Dumfries, Virginia, the oldest chartered town in the state of Virginia, and is part of the Washington, DC, metropolitan area. The church has grown from twelve members to serving over one thousand people.

Dr. Grier has run several businesses and is a successful investor. He has served as senior editor of *BothSides* magazine, a publication that addresses the tough cultural issues of the day and was originally an annual insert into *The Washington Post*. Dr. Grier studied business administration at Howard University and earned a master's of education from Regent

University. He also has earned a doctorate in practical ministry from Wagner Leadership Institute.

Dr. Grier has received many awards and commendations, including the 2005 Defender of Marriage Award, presented by the Marriage Alliance in Washington, DC. In the late 90's, he received letters from as far away as members of the House of Lords in England, as well as from members of the United States Congress, for his groundbreaking articles on the slavery crisis in the Sudan.

Dr. Grier has served on various boards and has been a regular consultant to members of the United States Congress and several state and local officials. He has had frequent invitations to the White House and has met with Heads of State and Christian leaders from around the world.

Dr. Grier has traveled to numerous countries and has become a respected leader in the Washington, DC, metropolitan area. He has appeared in *Ebony* magazine and *The Washington Post*, and has been featured on *The 700 Club*, Canada's *100 Huntley Street*, and in numerous other publications and programs. Hundreds of thousands have been impacted by his *Ministry Minute* broadcast, and now millions through the *Ministry Moment* aired on television.

Dr. Grier, his wife, and two sons reside in northern Virginia.

TO CONTACT THE AUTHOR

bishop@gracechurchva.org

For more information or to sign up to receive monthly Ministry Minute downloads, visit:

DerekGrier.com

ALSO AVAILABLE FROM DR. DEREK GRIER

A WOULD-BE BLACK MUSLIM RETURNS TO HIS college dormitory room and personally meets the man he so staunchly opposed, Jesus Christ.

In *Still Standing*, the author skillfully interweaves his twentieth-century story with that of the prophet Daniel, who lived over 2,500 years ago. The writing has such passion and rhythm that it seems to breathe in the reader's hand. This journey is not for the faint of heart. Grier tackles some hard questions about race and reveals the underside of religion. He is ruthlessly honest in his examination of himself, but he faces his personal demons squarely and ultimately triumphs.

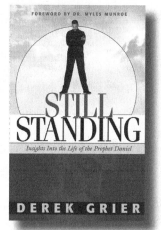

$7.99

Available online and at fine bookstores everywhere

enjoy both wit and wisdom, and all within an hour's worth of good reading. So read on!

—DON KROAH
105.1 FM WAVA
DON KROAH SHOW
DC METROPOLITAN AREA

Dr. Grier's book offers a refreshing and straightforward perspective to winning in life. It outlines tangible strategies to conquering goals and advancing toward personal destiny. It's a must-read!

—MATT ANDERSON
PRAISE 104.1 FM WRPS
THE MATT ANDERSON SHOW
DC METROPOLITAN AREA

Dr. Grier is a wealth of inspiration and wisdom. This book is a tremendous opportunity to discover power for living.

—DENISE HILL
MIDDAY HOST OF 1190 AM WLIB
NYC METROPOLITAN AREA
FORMER HOST OF THE SPIRIT, CHANNEL 33 XM SATELLITE

This book is a winner and I love it! Derek Grier's practical approach to applying the principles of life leaps over complicated philosophical and theological theories to deliver a people-friendly masterpiece that everyone will enjoy. This work is an inspiring source of daily motivation for the human heart.

—DR. MYLES MUNROE
SENIOR PASTOR, BAHAMAS FAITH MINISTRIES
NASSAU, BAHAMAS
CHAIRMAN, INTERNATIONAL THIRD WORLD
LEADERSHIP ASSOCIATION

Dr. Derek Grier has created a collection of insightful, pithy snapshots of where every Christian lives. He has covered a multitude of topics with bite-sized portions of spiritual insight. *60 Minutes of Wisdom's* seasoned and practical approach will not only make you think but also change. This book is a homerun!

—BISHOP HARRY R. JACKSON, JR.
SENIOR PASTOR, HOPE CHRISTIAN CHURCH,
WASHINGTON, DC, AREA
FOUNDER AND PRESIDENT, HIGH IMPACT
LEADERSHIP COALITION

If it's true that "brevity is the soul of wit," it can also be a source of real wisdom! In Dr. Derek Grier's book *60 Minutes of Wisdom*, you will